BLAZERS

MILITARY VEHICLES

U.S.
ARMY
HELICOPTERS

by Carrie A. Braulick

Reading Consultant:
Barbara J. Fox
Reading Specialist
North Carolina State University

Capstone
press

Mankato, Minnesota

Blazers is published by Capstone Press,
151 Good Counsel Drive, P.O. Box 669, Mankato, Minnesota 56002.
www.capstonepress.com

Library of Congress Cataloging-in-Publication Data
Braulick, Carrie A., 1975–
    U.S. Army helicopters / by Carrie A. Braulick.
    p. cm.—(Blazers—military vehicles)
    Includes bibliographical references and index.
    Summary: "Provides an overview of the design, uses, weapons,
and equipment of U.S. Army helicopters"—Provided by publisher.
    ISBN-13: 978-0-7368-5468-9 (hardcover)
    ISBN-10:0-7368-5468-1 (hardcover)
    1. Military helicopters—United States—Juvenile literature. 2.
United States. Army—Equipment and supplies—Juvenile literature. I.
Title. II. Series.
    UG1233.B73 2006
    623.74'6047—dc22   2005016446

Editorial Credits
Mandy Marx, editor; Thomas Emery, designer; Jo Miller, photo researcher/
    photo editor

Photo Credits
Corbis/Jack Novak, 18; Ramin Talaie, 17
DVIC/Christopher J. Varville, 27; MSGT Lance Cheung, cover, 9; MSGT
    Sabastian J. Sciotti, 7 (top); Raymond A. Barnard, 15 (top); SSGT
    Jerry Morrison, Jr., 20
Getty Images Inc./AFP/Darko Bandic, 26; AFP/Peter Drent, 10; Joe
    Raedle, 11; U.S. Air Force/Glenn Wilkewitz, 12
Photo by Ted Carlson/Fotodynamics, 5, 7 (bottom), 13, 15 (bottom),
    19, 21, 22–23, 25, 28–29

062011   006228WZVMI

**Capstone Press thanks Bradley Osterman, U.S. Army, for his
assistance with this book.**

TABLE OF CONTENTS

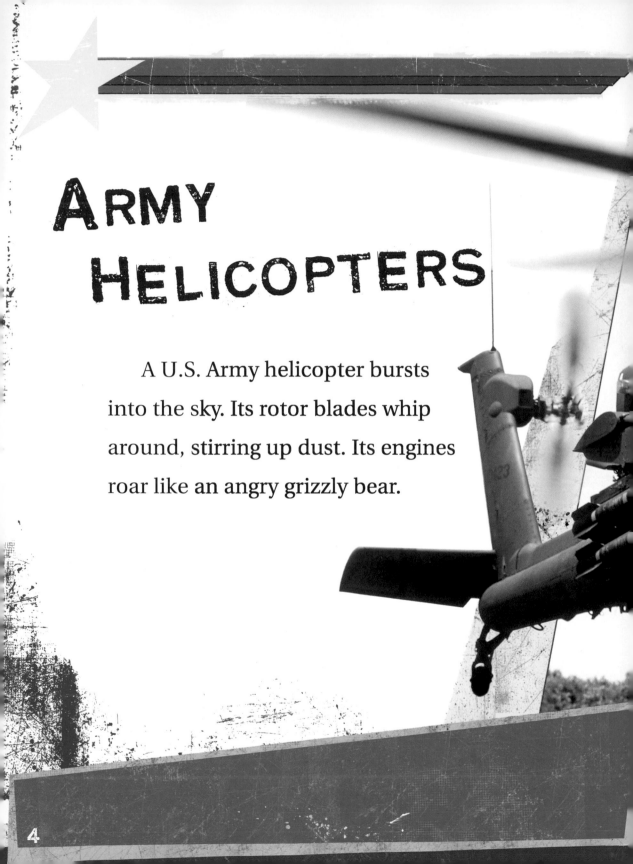

ARMY HELICOPTERS

A U.S. Army helicopter bursts into the sky. Its rotor blades whip around, stirring up dust. Its engines roar like an angry grizzly bear.

Army helicopters perform many jobs. Some helicopters blow up enemy targets from miles away. Others lift heavy loads quite easily.

DESIGN

Each Army helicopter is built
with different abilities. Apache attack
helicopters are small and fast. They
are hard for enemies to shoot down.

AH-64 APACHE

10

Chinook helicopters have large rotors and powerful engines. They carry loads as heavy as a fighter jet.

Black Hawk helicopters are bigger
than Apaches but smaller than Chinooks.
They can carry 11 soldiers. But Black
Hawks are small enough to travel quickly.

BLAZER FACT

The U.S. Navy, Coast Guard, and Air Force fly their own versions of the Black Hawk.

Kiowa helicopters have excellent systems for vision and communication. Pilots use the Kiowa to track enemy actions.

VISION SYSTEM

OH-58D KIOWA WARRIOR

WEAPONS AND EQUIPMENT

Machine guns on Army helicopters shoot bullets quickly. Some fire up to 2,000 bullets a minute.

Missiles stop even the toughest enemy tanks. Some missiles follow laser beams to their targets.

AGM-114 MISSILES

BLAZER FACT

The Apache helicopter carries more weapons than any other helicopter in the world.

CABLES

Transport helicopters have strong cables and hooks to carry loads. Attack helicopters have radar systems. Radar can keep track of 128 targets at a time.

RADAR

UH-60 BLACK HAWK

MAIN ROTOR

ENGINE

COCKPIT

LANDING GEAR

CABIN

TAIL ROTOR

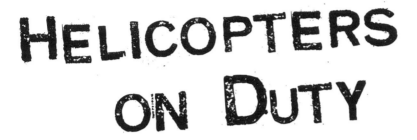

HELICOPTERS ON DUTY

A pilot and copilot fly Army
helicopters from the cockpit.
In some helicopters, other
crew members fire weapons.

Some helicopters go on combat missions. Others go on training or rescue missions. Each job shows the power of these fierce flying machines.

BLAZER FACT

Army helicopters on missions fly close to the ground. They hide behind trees and hills.

ON A MISSION!

GLOSSARY

bullet (BUL-it)—a small, pointed metal object fired from a gun

cable (KAY-buhl)—a thick wire or rope used for lifting heavy objects

cockpit (KOK-pit)—the area in front of a helicopter where the pilot and copilot sit

laser beam (LAY-zur BEEM)—a powerful, narrow ray of light

machine gun (muh-SHEEN GUN)—a large gun that fires bullets quickly

missile (MISS-uhl)—an explosive weapon that can fly long distances

radar (RAY-dar)—equipment that uses radio waves to locate and guide objects

rotor (ROH-tur)—machinery on a helicopter that spins a set of rotating blades

target (TAR-git)—something that is aimed or shot at

READ MORE

Dartford, Mark. *Helicopters.* Military Hardware in Action. Minneapolis: Lerner, 2003.

Englart, Mindi Rose. *Helicopters: From Start to Finish.* Made in the U.S.A. San Diego: Blackbirch Press, 2002.

Green, Michael, and Gladys Green. *Weapons Carrier Helicopters: The UH-60 Black Hawks.* War Machines. Mankato, Minn.: Capstone Press, 2005.

INTERNET SITES

FactHound offers a safe, fun way to find Internet sites related to this book. All of the sites on FactHound have been researched by our staff.

Here's how:

1. Visit *www.facthound.com*
2. Type in this special code **0736854681** for age-appropriate sites. Or enter a search word related to this book for a more general search.
3. Click on the **Fetch It** button.

FactHound will fetch the best sites for you!

INDEX